Balboa Press books may be ordered through booksellers or by contacting:

Balboa Press
A Division of Hay House
1663 Liberty Drive
Bloomington, IN 47403
www.balboapress.com
1 (877) 407-4847

Because of the dynamic nature of the Internet, any web addresses or links contained in this book may have changed since publication and may no longer be valid. The views expressed in this work are solely those of the author and do not necessarily reflect the views of the publisher, and the publisher hereby disclaims any responsibility for them.

Any people depicted in stock imagery provided by Thinkstock are models, and such images are being used for illustrative purposes only.
Certain stock imagery © Thinkstock.

ISBN: 978-1-5043-3054-1 (sc)
ISBN: 978-1-5043-3055-8 (e)

Library of Congress Control Number: 2015904787

Print information available on the last page.

Balboa Press rev. date: 03/31/2015

BALBOA.
PRESS
A DIVISION OF HAY HOUSE

# Four Seasons

## in a Garden

by

*Judy Carlson*

# Four Seasons
## in a Garden

by

*Judy Carlson*

*Also: "Reflections from a Garden"*
*"Life Lessons from a Garden"*

# Serenity in a Garden

Where the Lord is…is Holy

I am aware of God's presence in the garden. It is my place to meet with Him and have the thoughts and intentions of my heart judged. It is not for everyone. It may not be for you who look at this book but I have a desire to share my journey. If you have read last summer's "Reflections from a Garden" then you are aware of my illness and that I coped with my type of blood disorder by growing a rose garden in the desert and reflecting on the names of each rose.

It did not begin as a book, but rather a way for me to enjoy my life. Before I started to garden my dog Coco and I would go for a little walk every day up our country road. I wanted to leave a legacy of love and give back in some way but I wasn't sure how that would happen. I started to take a trash bag with me and as we walked we stopped and picked up the trash that others tossed out of their vehicles as they drove by. I was struck by the peace as we walked. We saw fields of alfalfa, and cows grazing. One walk I saw the grass had just been cut and it was laying in the field, surrendered to its fate. I too had surrendered to my fate. We saw all manner of birds: yellow-headed black birds, red winged black birds, meadowlarks, and California quail running the roads with their tiny babies. We saw black ibis gleaning in the fields, and of course sage sparrows.

Every day as we walked we picked up trash, I thought: "Well it's a small, simple thing but we are caring for our road." My heart was full of the joy of living and I searched for ways to enhance my caring. It was an uncertain diagnosis for me. I could have become very ill, very quickly or if I responded well to treatment I could remain stable. When you have that earthquake in your life I think that it is normal to want to make a positive impact of love before you die. I wanted to. I would ask on my walks: "Why have I been given this life, is there any unfinished business? Did I somehow miss my life's assignment?" Then one weekend I came home after a few days away to find that my neighbor had planted three rose bushes in my yard to cheer me up. They were lovely. I decided that I wanted more and more, so I eventually planted 50 roses.

The roses were then so beautiful that I would snap a picture of them when they were in full bloom. I was capturing their beauty for the moment. I struggled to live in the moment. I knew that remembering things past would lead to regret and looking to an uncertain future could produce worry, so I practiced living in the moment. I called myself back every time I tended to venture into another time zone. I eventually got the hang of it and would stay in the garden with my dog Coco at my side for hours.

Aware that God is outside of time and not bound by our schedules I felt His presence. He was there with me. I realized one afternoon that each rose was named, and thought of little reflections that accompanied their names. Finally as I began to write for the sake of my own failing memory it occurred to me that there were Bible scriptures that could be applicable for each rose. The garden had been so healing for me and joy-filled that I wanted to share it with anyone suffering illness. I wanted to share my journey in the hopes that even one person could identify and be comforted.

This book, "Four Seasons in a Garden" is not just about roses but also about my spring, summer, autumn and winter garden. There will be some flowers and reflections included that are not new to you. My time spent in the garden and my journey through illness and various other trials enabled me to see how precious life is. I am not experiencing the level of energy that I was so grateful for last summer. I am still here however, and still in the garden.

I need to make a disclaimer. I am not an expert gardener. I am not a Bible or wisdom literature expert. I am not a theologian. I am just a grateful heart who each day experiences the goodness of God in the universe. It took serious illness to wake me up. In the quiet and beauty of nature I began to see that we are all connected. We all play our part and we are all responsible for caring for and tending it. I invite you to come and journey with me into the Garden.

# Spring

## Hyacinth

The story of the hyacinth is a Greek tragedy. The gods Apollo and Zephyrus were fighting for the attention of beautiful Hyacinth. I think that all of our lives contain Greek tragedy at one time or another. We all have dying and rising moments - we are all tested by life. Unfortunate circumstances will come into our lives. It's inevitable. But we can learn from them, overcome them, move on from them, and turn them around for good. The story goes, as Hyacinth died the god Apollo turned a drop of his blood into the flower. The sacrifice of one yields beauty. Nothing that you ever say or do is wasted. I believe that all of our thoughts, intentions and actions, and also failures to act have eternal meaning and consequence. You matter greatly.

*"But, beloved, we are convinced of better things concerning you, and things that accompany salvation"*

*(Hebrews 6:9)*

# *Snapdragons*

These snapdragons were planted last fall. They were the last batch of flowers left in the nursery. They were small and ready to say: "lights out." I planted them in a bed near the house to give them as much protection as possible. Typically, the wind here can blow anywhere from 30 to 50 miles per hour. I hoped that the radiant heat from the house would also help them. I see all of nature as a part of God. They are not human or animal, but they are life. They have similar needs to us in that they respond to the warmth of the sun. They need drink and they show off most beautifully if they are fed with organic material (in other words, a healthy diet). They dance in the breeze. They are vibrant with a variety of colors. They cycle through life, experiencing all of the four seasons. They are also selfless in sharing beauty. I see them as a pure gift from God.

*"All good giving and every perfect gift is from above coming down from the Father of Lights."*

(James 1:17)

# Giant Allium

This flower is made up of many florets. Individual, distinct parts of the flower come together to create something beautiful. Similarly, I think that we are many parts coming together as God's beautiful creation. This spring while the daffodils and tulips were showing off, the giant allium was … kind of homely. It just looked like a ball on a tall stick. I was afraid that I had made a mistake planting it in my spring garden. However, while the others were retiring the allium began to bloom, tall, purple and beautiful, and its life duration was long. Now, as it too begins to fade into summer I see that it is transparent. You can see right through the flower. I also feel more transparent at this time in my life. The facades fall away as we grow in time and grace. We can no longer indulge in pretense but rather be seen for who we have become in heart and soul.

> *"My frame was not hidden from Thee, when I was made in secret, and skillfully wrought in the depths of the earth. Thine eyes have seen my unformed substance; and in Thy book they were all written, the days that were ordained for me."*

(Psalm139: 15,16)

# *Tulips*

The amazing thing about these tulips was the extent to which they responded to the warmth of the sun. My friend Sheila once told me that it was important in life to always be open to the possibilities. My son was Special Forces in the Army and he told me that one of the Special Operations mottos was, "He Who Dares, Wins." I made a decision when I became ill to be open to what God and life had in store for me. I was going to dare to live every day to the fullest. Now, obviously a full day displayed itself in different ways but I followed my heart, and that almost always meant that I went outside. I went outside to feel the warmth of the sun, the wind against my cheek, listen to the singing of the birds, touch the earth with my hands, and sometimes smell something sweet. Choose to live through all of your senses.

*"Open my eyes that I may behold wonderful things"*

*(Psalm119: 18)*

# Purple Pansies

The endurance of these delicate little flowers fascinated me. They can be planted when it is still too cold for so many other types of flowers. Our spring weather here in Nevada is so fickle. It can be 65 or 70 degrees in the afternoon and then dip down to nighttime freeze. I was impatient some days and would plant a new flower only to lose it to frost. The pansies however were tried and true - faithful to be well in the morning garden. We also have an unrealized strength. It remains deep inside of us until a life situation calls it forth. We may be *wonderfully and fearfully made*, (Ps: 139:14) and so I believe we are, but our bodies are also delicate. The pansies represented to me the paradox in life where there can be strength in apparent weakness.

# *Lily*

These gorgeous lilies shout in the garden. Let your light shine for the entire world to see! I see these lilies as beautiful, confident, uninhibited flowers. They are magnificent additions to the garden and they come in a variety of forms and colors. I have yellow day lilies and the white Easter lilies. We all hide a part of ourselves. We can be shy and afraid that if people see who we really are, it will be a disaster. We all give our power over to someone else at one time or another. It's a tough walk being confident in your own color and not wanting to seem prideful. The connotation for the name lily is shining light. The meaning is purity. It will be pure joy allowing your life to flow from your soul - not your ego.

*"Let your light shine before men in such a way that they may see your good works, and glorify your Father who is in heaven."*

*(Matthew 5:16)*

# Alyssum...(Carpet of Snow)

These tender delicate little flowers are annuals. They do their job only for a season. They are content to allow other flowers to feature more beautifully by being near them or surrounding them. I think of alyssum as a flower with the quality of kindness. Last year I planted some near rocks and I noticed that they soften and climb up the rock. This spring I planted them all around the boarder of a large flowerbed. I can't wait for them to catch each other and join hands. They are like fractals. Each small flower becomes a bouquet, which then looks like the pattern of the larger flower. They also have a lovely scent and attract bees.

*"What is desirable in a man is his kindness."*

*(Proverbs 19:22)*

*Osteospermum*

This lovely addition is an African daisy. It comes in purple, lavender or white. It is a sun loving flower and very forgiving of harsh conditions. Once again, it is a flower perfect for our Nevada climate. I think it is a flower deserving of a place of honor in my garden for tolerating heat and draught. It is forgiving, one of the most difficult of qualities. I will speak for myself and say that I now, in my 60's, know that the act of forgiveness is one that must flow from the heart and soul. The human ego is abhorrent to forgiving. It is the ego's job to protect the pretense that we are too important to allow injury or insult. Let us be tolerant, and forgiving. It is the healthiest attitude for you and for me.

*Then Peter came and said to Him, "Lord how often shall my brother sin against*
*me and I forgive him?" Jesus said, "I say seventy times seven."*

*(Matthew18: 21)*

# *Delosperma Lavender Ice*

This lavender ice is a ground cover perfect for Nevada. It is content with little amounts of water and happy to grow in sand. Lucky for the plant those features are exactly what I can offer. The West always struggles with draught and we live in a prehistoric lakebed - check and check! It is a perennial so to my surprise it popped right up this spring. It looks fragile but it obviously has fortitude. This is a humble flower. It does not stretch up to the sky like the iris or allium. It creeps along the ground, which I always think of as humility. Humility is knowing exactly who you are before God.

*"Humble yourself in the presence of the Lord, and He will lift you up."*

*(James 4:10)*

# Salvia

There are hundreds of different types of salvias commonly known as sage. They will continue to bloom all summer right up until frost. The salvia or sage is of the mint family. This plant was grown for its healing capability as an herb. I draw a connection between sage as a person of profound wisdom and sage as healing. Proverbs 2:10 says: "For wisdom will enter your heart, and knowledge will be pleasant to your soul."

Job 28:12: "But where can wisdom be found? And where is the place of understanding?" I submit to you that I found God in the garden and with Him, small amounts of wisdom and understanding.

If there is healing in the mint herb than there is also healing for the soul in wisdom. Take wisdom where you find it. The diversity of the created world is vast and so are the opportunities to grow on your journey. I will say, however, that quiet and stillness will be necessary for your connection. It is in the still, small voice that God speaks.

*Then the Lord said, "Go outside and stand on the mountain*
*before the Lord; the Lord will be passing by."*

*(1 Kings19:11)*

# Summer

*Pink Iceberg*

This rose is a certainty in my garden. It endured our coldest nights and now makes an offering of huge numbers of blooms. Truly it is a little showstopper. It apparently does just as well if potted, so if you are restricted from caring for a larger rose garden this rose bush is for you. My intention in writing, 'Reflections from a Garden' and now this third volume is to encourage and inspire you. My journey of illness took me on a path outside to a garden. I want you to know that you are not alone, that we all journey together in some respect. We are fearfully and wonderfully made but that is no guarantee of perfect health for a life span. I pray and wish for you who read this book that life's challenges will never get you down. That you will go into the quiet, reach deep inside and find hope and live it everyday.

*"For I know the plans I have for you declares the Lord, plans for*
*welfare, to give you a future, and for hope...."*

(Jeremiah 29:11)

# *Elizabeth*

There is much meaning in a name. Everything about Elizabeth is lovely, delicate and feminine. The name Elizabeth is Hebrew for "Oath of God."

It is that God thought of us, that we exist at all, and we are sustained by His love for us. He conceived of us before we were conceived in our Mothers.

Throughout scripture, names matter and are sometimes changed to illustrate the transformation of the person. Abram became Abraham, Simon became Peter, and Sarai became Sarah. I believe that God whispers our name into our soul as life begins. It is the most intimate of acts, sharing breath with us. We are told in scripture to lay up our treasure in heaven and also that there is the promise of a new heavenly name.

*Whoever has ears ought to hear what the Spirit says… to him who overcomes…*

*I will give him a white stone, and a new name written on the*
*stone which no one knows but he who receives it.*

(Revelation 2:17)

# Wild Blue Yonder

This ruby red, purple rose has clusters of ruffled petals. It is so perfect for our area of Nevada that it is almost shameful for me to write about. It could have been named appropriately for the wild blue of the Nevada sky. Our clean blue skies can boast of well over three hundred days a year of sunshine. We have a military air station here where on any given day you can hear the sound of freedom over head. Since I started spending so much time outside with my roses I couldn't help but also appreciate the scenes that would drift by in the heavens. It is critical when you are dealing with any life trial that you be present to the moment and not drifting into another time zone. Train yourself to be alert and centered on each moment. The garden and my roses have been that for me but use whatever lifts your heart and mind to stay positive.

*"A cheerful heart is good medicine, but a crushed spirit dries up the bones"*

(Proverbs 15:13)

# *Sunshine Daydream*

This is an heirloom rose. Sunshine daydream has such a happy welcoming color and very faithful to be stunning in the morning. In the quiet of the morning I worship God's name. I lift my voice to praise Him. I chose to be in my garden because to me it is holy ground. It is where I can remove my shoes and seek the living God. I go out to look for Him among the beautiful ways in which He leaves clues to His nature. I see God in the colors, in the lovely delicate forms of the flowers. I hear him in the sounds. I sense Him in the fragrance of the roses and the earth. I see, feel, and hear the miracles of the Universe unfolding before me, in the garden.

*"So I will bless Thee as long as I live; I will lift up my hands in Thy*
*name …and my mouth offers praises with joyful lips".*

(Psalm 63:4-5)

# *Peace*

This is one of those roses that can take your breath away. I am not the first person to see in the rose a metaphor for life. The incredible beauty, its colors and the softness of the petals and how delicate and sensitive it can be. My roses require attention to thrive - love as it were. The more time you are able to spend with them the greater the reward in terms of their performance and beauty. However, along with the delicacy and beauty existing on the same rose, are thorns and the opportunities for injury. The chemo medicine that I take thins my blood so every time I approach without caution I am pricked and I bleed. It is not just me who can suffer for a wrong move in the garden. The wind here in northern Nevada can whip my rose garden into a dance, but as they move the thorns damage the bush. They are responsible for their own injury. Can the same not be said of us?

*"be not afraid but speak, and hold not thy peace for I am with thee..."*

(Acts18:9)

# Sugar Moon

Sugar Moon is a particularly delicate and beautiful rose. Its fragrance is indeed sweet and I also noticed in the garden that it seemed more vulnerable. That may be a truth of nature - that the more beautiful and delicate, the more susceptible. I know with all the gene research and therapies that are now being explored our vulnerabilities may decrease with time. Even though we are body, mind and spirit, my garden reflections are primarily targeted for the soul - that compartment within us specifically made for God and that shines in our eyes when we love, forgive, serve and live in gratitude. Life is a sweet gift.

*"The ordinances of the Lord are true, all of them just…sweeter also than honey from the comb."*

(Psalm 19:10)

# *Double Delight*

What an incredible beauty this rose has become. Its nature is doubly beautiful with pure radiant white and deep red blended together at the edges. It has been in my garden for two years but this October as our desert heat began to cool this rose became magnificent. The conditions in the garden were perfect for just a brief time for double delight to be the best that it was created to be. I challenge you to look for those moments and circumstances in your life where you are your authentic self. Put gentleness, compassion, kindness, humility, patience and peace into practice as often as you can. Judy Garland once said, "Always be a first rate version of yourself, instead of a second rate version of somebody else."

# About Face

This orange rose in my garden is faithful and lovely. It is a grandiflora rose and somewhat unusual for the changes in color it undergoes. We too undergo changes in color. It opens to a core of a bronze orange and lightens as its petals open. The fragrance is even very distinct. We burn brightly in our youth. We have so much energy and enthusiasm for the future. We can't wait to experience everything life has to offer. As we grow throughout our journey, we mellow and learn growing in wisdom, grace, patience and peace. It took illness for me to change colors - to view the world differently. Some might think that my health problems were a negative thing in my life but ….

*"All things work together for good for those who love the Lord*
*and are called according to His purpose."*

(Romans 8:28)

# *Brandy*

This brandy rose may well be the most delicious rose in my garden. It is easy to linger over its color, form and fragrance. There are some things in life that exist purely to be beautiful and this rose is one of them. The gifts in nature are always there for the taking if we only have eyes to see. It is apricot in color and in our warmer climate it promises to have huge blooms.

I was hard pressed to make room in my garden for brandy, I already had 50 roses to care for. I dug a little corner in the back, next to the house not aware of the quality of this rose. Sometimes the best and most beautiful things in our lives are overlooked. I would recommend here making a list of the little thing that give you pause and make you smile.

*"Do you have eyes and not see"*

(Mark 8:18)

# Koco Loco

This is such a unique rose. It buds perfectly as a mild chocolate brown and then opens in shades of light lavender. It is transformed. We are also transformed in life. Health professionals tell us that the elements that make up our bodies are continuously renewed. Whatever your age, realize that some of the cells that make up your body are many years younger. My health *dis*-ease was an unexpected trauma to me. I was shaken awake! It was unclear in the beginning how well I would respond to treatment and all that mattered in those early days was the health of my soul. I wanted my life's journey to end having mattered.

*"Do not conform yourself to this age but be transformed by the renewal of your mind that you may discern what is the will of God, what is good and pleasing and perfect."*

(Romans 12:2)

# Fall into Autumn

I find that the autumn is a special time of reflection. I often get very melancholy in the fall. The garden displays its strongest and boldest colors yet, but the morning chill suggests time is short. The garden has come to represent to me the cycle that is written encoded in the Universe. The beginning of every story shouts eventually for an ending. The fact that fall colors are bold and strong is no surprise to me. It is as if the journey to mature has taken the flowers through incredible trials. The heat and intense sunshine, wind, and draught, powdery mildew and all manner of insect attacks are typical weather characteristics to northern Nevada. The soil here is not really soil it is sand and offers up no nutrition for a garden.

I drew parallels in my previous garden reflection books between my flowers, especially my roses and my own journey with illness. Their beauty inspired me in soul and enlivened all my senses. I became fully alive in the garden. I was able to forget about my blood disorder and keep active in body, mind, and spirit. I was able to be present for every moment spent in the garden, not regretting anything past or worrying about anything in the future.

As this 2014 growing season draws to a close, I wish to share with you the joy and wisdom that I found in my garden. I titled this season's chapter, *Fall into Autumn* because I wish to share with you the peace I have found in falling, the peace that hides in surrender.

# *Dahlia*

These flowers were a complete surprise. I started to garden on the advice of a friend and once I had planted as many roses as the yard would accept I began to look forward to new challenges. The dahlia is a flower with specific needs. The effort in the spring is minimal but the reward is great! They do however require unique care and treatment to make it through a desert winter.

I can now understand what the desert has to offer. Many people seeking spiritual experiences and wisdom have looked to the desert. The three monotheistic religious denominations originated in desert lands. It is not a comfortable, easygoing existence that builds character. Our true self requires the fire of trials to burn away the dross, the greater the effort the more beautiful the flower.

*"Not only that, but we even boast of our afflictions, knowing*
*that affliction produces...proven character...."*

(Romans 5:3)

# *Gazania*

This tough little plant endures poor soil, baked conditions, and drought and still produces color and daisy-like flowers from summer to frost. Its colors are perfect in a fall garden with bold orange, yellow, and gold. The endurance of this little flower takes me to a reflection on my life's struggles. I want to share with you just a bit of my background. I come from an alcoholic violent family. My hiding place as a little girl was under our dining room table. My trials as an adult are unique to me but not in the sense that I am alone. Life with all its complexities happens to us all. I do not look for sympathy but want you to know that I am like you. Please know that you have the power to choose. You are a unique and incredible soul who can learn and be grateful for every trial.

*"Because the afflicted and the needy sigh, now will I arise," says*
*the Lord; "I will grant safety to him who longs for it."*

Psalm 12:6

# Chrysanthemum

The name "chrysanthemum" is derived from Latin for gold flower. They originated in Asia and there are about 40 species. This plant is synonymous with autumn. It pops up everywhere - in gardens, in nurseries, in grocery stores, and on porches this time of year. I like to include a small tidbit of information about each flower as I believe it is fun to continue learning as I have throughout my garden journey. This bright yellow mum is hard to miss in the garden. I have pink, rust, white and purple mums. It has taken all spring and summer for the chrysanthemum to flower. As the nights here grew colder, I patiently waited for these plants to bloom. We do not all mature in spirit and soul at the same rate. What joy would there be in that? We can celebrate the fruits of patience as we achieve it with ourselves. How can we gift something to another when we do not yet possess it? Be patient with yourself. Love yourself. You are wonderful - a miracle of creation.

*"I give you thanks that I am fearfully and wonderfully made"*

Psalm 139:14

# Marigolds

These annuals are multi purpose. They are bright and beautiful in color. They are easy to grow as a border or interspersed in a vegetable garden to discourage insects. There are several varieties of marigolds: marsh, French, Mexican, African, and desert to name a few. When I drive up our street, the marigolds are the first to greet me in the front yard. Greeting with friendly faces and easy smiles - that is what marigolds represent to me. The beauty of the flowers in my garden has been so healing for me. It is no accident that when people are ill or in the hospital, we think to bring them flowers. I have recommended having a flower garden to cheer you, maybe even heal you, but I know not everyone has a yard to accommodate 50 roses. My Mom had a few pots on her apartment balcony and she loved her hens & chicks. There is great joy in nurturing something beautiful.

*"we are writing this so that our joy may be complete"*

(1 John 1:4)

# *Coneflower*

This coneflower is named Aloha. There is a real conflict within this flower. Speaking to the gentler side of coneflowers, they attract bees and butterflies. It is always a gift to see a butterfly float in the garden making a general inspection. There is, however, another side to these Echinacea. They are prickly. The tall stocks of the plant have fine hairs that bristle at you if touched. I suppose that is why they claim to be deer proof. They remind me that we all have two faces. It can be a difficult thing to journey with others but the truth is that we can only grow if we allow ourselves to be seen and revealed in the eyes of others. We cannot fully know or be known without the help of family and friends. It is not in our best interest to journey alone. We must let others walk with us. I am placing a small scripture quote here but please take the time with this flower to read the entire story of the road to Emmaus.

"And it happened that while he was with them at table…their eyes were opened"

(Luke 24:30,31)

# Coreopsis

This wonderful flower is true to last in the garden from spring into fall as long as you are willing to deadhead the spent flowers. I know that in my Spring Life Lessons book I talked about this truth but I am going to suggest it once again to emphasize the importance. When you snip off the spent flower head, another new bloom comes to take its place. In the plant it ensures fullness of growth and beautiful fresh flowers. It matters not whether you deal with illness; loss of a job, friend or relative; a trauma to yourself or someone you love. You must grieve, snip away the pain, and move forward. You must embrace your life, loves, and losses to be wholly healed.

*"He heals the brokenhearted and binds up their wounds"*

(Psalm 147:3)

# Kalanchoe

This succulent produces multiple clusters of little flowers. It is an annual in the garden, as it won't tolerate our cold winter nights. It is most common as an indoor houseplant preferring temperatures above 55F. I love the variety of names given to this species of plant. They are: velvetleaf, devil's backbone, Mexican hat, donkey ears, pies from heaven, and panda plant just to name a few. This plant obviously inspires imagination. My journey in the garden was inspirational for me. As I was able to quiet my life, mind, and soul, I became aware of images and concepts never acknowledged by me before. It is critical when ill to follow your doctor's treatment plan but there are other things you can do for yourself. You can listen to music, accept hugs, have someone read to you, and imagine yourself completely healthy. You can form mental images of yourself happy and placed in the Universe perfectly.

*But for you who revere my name, the sun of righteousness will rise with healing in its rays.*

(Malachi 4:2)(NIV)

# *Lavender*

It is late October and as I write this reflection my lavender is still beautiful. The life expectancy of the lavender plant is ten years so it is recommended that you plant another every few years. The one I have in my garden is three years old. It offers up beauty, color, fragrance, and a diversity of life as it invites bees and butterflies to dine. I have many types of plants and flowers in my garden but one can't help having favorites. My fifty roses are special but so is any plant that endures the trials and the test of time in the desert. I believe that we all have an untapped reservoir of strength and courage. Like the peace that hides in surrender, your courage waits for a life experience to call it forth. Embrace your life and be grateful for it. Practice being grateful for just one thing everyday and like the lavender you will attract happiness!

*"All good giving and every perfect gift is from above, coming down from*
*the Father of lights, with whom there is no shadow of turning."*

(James 1:17)

# *Dianthus*

This lovely faithful little flower is a member of the carnation family. The name dianthus means divine flower. I have several colors in my garden and they are wonderful to bloom from spring all the way to frost. The garden is most beautiful when you spend time in it with love. Please remember that there is a part of each one of us that is divine. We are not pieces of tissue that accidentally materialized. We are the children of God. "See how great a love the Father has bestowed on us, that we should be called children of God." 1John 3:1. I ask you to stop for a moment and think of how much you love your children. Now, multiply that by infinity.

The seasons of your life come and go but happiness is a state of mind - not a state of circumstance. Find hope in your heart and live it everyday.

*"and hope does not disappoint, because the love of God has been poured*
*out within our hearts through the Holy Spirit who was given to us."*

(Romans 5:5)

# Winchester Cathedral

It's a cold November Saturday morning. It has been a very rough week. By the end of the week I was as humbled and weak as this rose in my garden. I share with you because I have now written four garden books full of starry-eyed optimism and I need to share that the journey I take is possibly like yours - fraught with trials, stresses, and sometimes heart breaking sadness. As the tears trickled down my face it was one of my son's dogs Rocinante who never left my side. His eyes were locked onto my face as we sat together. What a wonderful wee soul he has.

*"But we have this treasure in earthen vessels, so that the surpassing greatness of the power will be of God and not from ourselves; we are afflicted in every way, but not crushed; perplexed, but not despairing; persecuted, but not forsaken; struck down but not destroyed"*

(2 Corinthians 4:8,9)

# Winter

It is a cold January day in the garden. Our Sierra Nevada mountains are blanketed with beautiful white crystals of snow. This garden, however, is in a valley and more often than not we get fog that freezes. It's called Pogonip. Pogonip is a Shoshone word for the ice crystals that form in the fog that settles in the mountain valleys of the west. When this weather phenomenon visits my state it usually remains for several weeks.

The skies grow dark with fog and there is no sunshine. Because the fog seals in our valley, the air is chilly with ice crystals. It sets up an environment begging for reflection. Everything about the landscape becomes grey. Grey is a color neither black nor white. It is a neutral, an in-between. Most, if not all, of my adult life has been lived in-between: in-between engagement and marriage, in-between getting pregnant and having the baby, in-between kindergarten and graduation and in-between youth and wisdom. Think of the wonder filled experiences that take place in the in-between. Winter is a perfect season for it with all the celebrations and activities designed to bring families together. The time even manipulates us. The early darkness sends us indoors for a hot meal and cookies. The roses are not entirely hiding - they can be spotted on the cheeks of little ones. The earth is at rest.

"There is an appointed time for everything, and a time for every affair under the heavens."

(Ecclesiastes 3:1)

It's odd for me to see my lavender lying down. It may well be the busiest plant in my garden. It must be hospitable and welcoming as it is never alone. The bees and the butterflies are constant companions. You can see that the weight of the ice crystals is a burden and yet it is the natural extension of a cycle of service. I remember my parents who worked their entire lives to make a home for us. I remember the generations past who had diabetes before insulin, and arthritis before NSAIDs and colds and flu before decongestants. I remember my Dad never ever missing a day of work and my Mom who worked as a sales clerk and then took care of us all. I think of all the families who live their incredible lives in the *in-between* now and again making a time for rest. They do not bow low with burden, but rather in humility - possibly the dearest and loveliest of virtues for a life well lived. I believe that those who live in humility live in the presence of God.

*"Humble yourselves, therefore, under the mighty hand of God*
*so that at the proper time he may exalt you,"*

(1 Peter 5:6)

I sum up this chapter on the winter garden by reminding you that the power to live a full, happy, and healthy life resides within you.

So I close Four Seasons in a Garden with a thank you and grateful heart for all of you who have joined me on this garden journey. I feel a connection that transcends physical contact. I know that if you have a love of God in nature and see His fingerprint in life, you are my travelling companions. I wish you health, love and peace.

# Acknowledgements

For my dear parents, Michael Joseph and Marie Alma, who taught me that life is worth fighting for.

*"Love Never Fails."*

1Corinthians 13:8

Your Thoughts

# Your Thoughts

# Your Thoughts

# Your Thoughts

Printed in the United States
By Bookmasters